MAN DANGLI

Three Short Plays

By MURRAY SCHISGAL

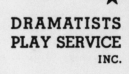

DRAMATISTS
PLAY SERVICE
INC.

Dramatists Play Service

New
PLAYS

SWEET SUE
THE COMMON PURSUIT
ELEEMOSYNARY
AMERICAN DREAMS
BOUNCERS
PHAEDRA
THE MADERATI
LILY DALE
RUNNING ON EMPTY
T BONE N WEASEL
MRS. CALIFORNIA
FUN & NOBODY
MAN DANGLING
THE WIDOW CLAIRE

Inquiries Invited

DRAMATISTS PLAY SERVICE, INC.

440 Park Avenue South   New York, N. Y. 10016

NEW

Plays

STEEL MAGNOLIAS

THE LUCKY SPOT

THE DREAMER EXAMINES HIS PILLOW

BODIES, REST, AND MOTION

HOW TO SAY GOODBYE

JACOB'S LADDER

PASTA

MR. 80%

TRACERS

DANGER: MEMORY!

VANISHING ACT

PROGRESS

THE DREAM COAST

JITTERS

DRAMATISTS PLAY SERVICE, INC.

440 PARK AVENUE SOUTH   **NEW YORK, N.Y. 10016**

MAN DANGLING

Three Short Plays

By MURRAY SCHISGAL

**DRAMATISTS
PLAY SERVICE
INC.**

CONTENTS

To David Kugelman

MAN DANGLING was first presented in a public reading at The Apple Corps Theatre, New York City, John Raymond, Artistic Director, with the following cast:

THE CONSEQUENCES OF GOOSING

JESSIE BLOOM........................ Barbara Sinclair
MORTON BLOOM .... Michael Tolan

HOW WE REACHED AN IMPASSE
ON NUCLEAR ENERGY

DENNIS .... Michael Tolan
ROSALIND .... Deidre Westervelt

(INTERMISSION)

74 GEORGIA AVENUE

JOSEPH WATSON .... Charles Turner
MARTY ROBBINS .... Bob Dishy

THE CONSEQUENCES
OF GOOSING

THE CONSEQUENCES OF GOOSING

SCENE: A West Side co-op: the living room.

TIME: Summer: late afternoon.

AT RISE: Jessie Bloom is on the phone.

JESSIE. *(Into phone.)* Wait. Wait a second. Will you wait one second, Harold! I can't believe what I'm hearing! I can't! Will you let me catch my breath? Please. *(A short beat.)* All right. Now. If I understood you correctly, Harold, you said that Morton, my husband Morton, was picked up by the police ... for ... for as you put it ... goosing a young girl on Columbus Avenue. Is that ... correct? *(A short beat; repeats what she hears.)* And ... he was released on his own recognizance ... until Wednesday ... when there is to be a formal court hearing. *(A short beat; repeats what she hears.)* And ... he has to bring with him a psychiatric report. Yes. Go on. Unfortunately ... there was a photographer in the courtroom ... the entire matter ... no doubt ... will appear in the morning newspapers. *(A short beat.)* Is that it? He didn't disgrace us any further? *(A short beat.)* Of course I'll be supportive! Of course I will! I'm married to the man for twenty-two years! I'm the mother of his son who, ironically enough, was chosen today to be editor of the Law Review at Harvard University! *(Voice rising.)* What I don't understand, what I will never understand, is why Morton had to ... had to goose a young girl on Columbus Avenue! Why? In heaven's name, why? Did I ever, ever refuse him anything? Did I ever say no to him, to whatever he asked, even if I was deathly ill and nauseous to my stomach?

Harold, you are missing the point! The point is that he didn't have to goose her. He has a wife at home! He has a faithful, devoted ... *(A short beat.)* How old is she? Seventeen? *(Each word emphasized.)* He goosed a seventeen-year-old girl? Oh, that is disgusting. That is ... *(A short beat.)* Of course I'll be supportive! Didn't I say ... Harold, how could he have done such a thing? He's a lawyer, an attorney at law. Did he lose his mind? Is he having a nervous breakdown? *(A short beat.)* Please try to understand what a ... what a shock this has been to me. I know how close you two are. *(Repeats what she hears.)* Yes. Boyhood buddies; law school classmates; and ... for many years members of the law firm of Whitmore, Fenton and Priestly. Yes. You have been a good friend and I trust ... *(Someone is opening the entrance door with a key.)* Wait! Wait! He's here! He's at the door! I'll call you back later! *(She hangs up; quickly sits down on sofa, picks up a magazine, crosses leg and pretends all is as it should be. Morton Bloom enters. He is wearing a suit; carries a briefcase. Except for perhaps a slight weariness in his neck muscles, there is nothing out of the ordinary about his appearance.)*

MORTON. *(Crosses to desk.)* Hi.

JESSIE. *(Without raising her eyes from magazine.)* Hi.

MORTON. How are you?

JESSIE. Fine.

MORTON. *(Puts briefcase on desk; looks through a few pieces of mail.)* You had a nice day?

JESSIE. Yes. Very pleasant. You?

MORTON. Fine. Fine. A ... very nice day. *(He moves to sit in armchair, R. He whistles, taps his fingers on armrest, looks out the window.)*

JESSIE. *(Eyes on magazine.)* Can I get you anything?

MORTON. No. No, thank you. *(Whistles; taps fingers.)*

JESSIE. I thought we'd go out for dinner tonight.

MORTON. Excellent idea. I'm all for it. *(Whistles; taps fingers.)*

JESSIE. How do chichimongas at Caramba's sound to you?

MORTON. Wonderful. We can have margaritas beforehand. *(Whistles; taps fingers.)*

10

JESSIE. *(Closes magazine; now in a grim tone of voice.)* You are going to sit there and you are not going to say anything!

MORTON. I beg your pardon.

JESSIE. You are not going to say anything about being arrested, about being taken down to the police station and being released on your own recognizance, or about having to appear at a formal court hearing next Wednesday and bring with you a psychiatric report! *(Morton stares at her thoughtfully an instant, then turns away and whistles, tapping his fingers on armrest. Throws magazine down on floor; rises.)* How could you do this to me? How? *You goosed* a seventeen-year-old girl on Columbus Avenue? In broad daylight? In front of hundreds of people? Is that possible, Morton? Is *it* possible?

MORTON. *(Clears his throat.)* What ... time would you, uhhh, like to go for the chichimongas at Caramba's?

JESSIE. Don't do this to me! Please! I'm your wife, your wife of twenty-two years! Douglas was chosen editor of the Law Review today! I'm not a witch! I'm not a monster! I'm your wife and I ... I have no life but your life! *(Sobbing she sits on floor at his side and buries her head in his lap. Morton hesitates, then pats her, consolingly.)*

MORTON. It's a mistake. A miscarriage of justice. I did nothing wrong, Jessie; nothing. Someone might be setting me up for a reason I can't fathom at the moment. But ... I swear to you, I did not lay a finger on that girl; not a finger.

JESSIE. *(Sits upright; wipes her eyes with handkerchief.)* Will you tell me what ... happened? How ... ?

MORTON. *(Rises; moves to stare out of window.)* I walked home from the office, as I do every day, up Fifty-seventh Street, across the Circle into Columbus Avenue. It had been an exceptionally good day for me. Harold and I had settled a two million dollar lawsuit and Whitmore congratulated us; he said there has been some talk of our becoming full partners. You can imagine how happy that made me. I was feeling wonderful. I stopped off on Sixty-third Street and bought a tofutti ice-cream cone. It was the first I ever had. It was delicious. Further on I stopped in front of the Charivari men's store on Seventy-second Street and stared at a green woolen

11

cardigan sweater that I thought extremely handsome. I made a mental note of buying it Saturday. I moved on. I remember thinking of our trip to Sicily this fall when, out of the corner of my eye, I saw this young girl, with one foot up on a bench ... It was on the museum side of Columbus Avenue, at Eightieth Street. She was tying the shoelace on her sneaker. I didn't see her clearly. I wasn't even paying any attention to her. But as I passed her ... Suddenly ... From out of nowhere ... Two policemen jumped out of their patrol car, grabbed me ... People gathered around, there was a crowd of people, and before I could protest or ... or give them identification ... I was hustled into the patrol car and driven off. *(A short beat.)* I phoned Harold from the West Eighty-second Street police station.

JESSIE. *(Seated in armchair by now.)* You didn't touch her?

MORTON. *(Turns to her.)* I didn't touch her. I wasn't near enough to touch her. The only thing I can think of is that from the policemen's perspective, as I was passing her, it might have *appeared* as if I touched her. That's the only...

JESSIE. What did the girl say?

MORTON. The girl?

JESSIE. The one you were supposed to have ... touched.

MORTON. Nothing. She didn't scream. She didn't cry. She was a very cool and collected young lady.

JESSIE. What did she say?

MORTON. She said I ... goosed her.

JESSIE. How is it possible that she said you ... goosed her and you say you didn't ... goose her.

MORTON. Perhaps, perhaps when I passed her I created a wind ... a wind or a sort of breeze that she mistook for a goose when in reality I didn't goose her at all!

JESSIE. But you weren't close enough to her, isn't that right?

MORTON. Yes. But perhaps ... if I leaned over ... you could argue that it *was* physically possible for me to ... to goose her. However, I did not lean over and I did not ... *(The phone rings two or three times before Jessie picks it up.)*

JESSIE. *(Into phone.)* Yes? *(A short beat; flustered.)* Mr. Whitmore,

12

I ... Yes, fine. Of course. Yes, we are. He's right here. *(She holds the phone up to Morton. He takes it from her.)*

MORTON. *(A deep breath; then into phone.)* Yes, Ben. *(A short beat.)* Did you want to speak to me about ... anything in particular? *(A short beat.)* Oh. Harold filled you in, did he? I was ... hoping he would. *(Looking to Jessie with a worried expression.)* Is it necessary to ... Ben, the entire episode is an egregious error. There is no basis ... I will clear the matter up to your satisfaction, I promise. If it does get into the newspapers, I will ask for a public apology from the young lady, from the police department and from City Hall as well. *(A short beat.)* I can appreciate your concern. Should our clients react adversely ... Yes, but ... We could ... *(Mops brow.)* No. I wouldn't withold my consent. If you think it in the best interest of the firm, you can assure our clients privately ... *(A short beat.)* Ben, I wasn't planning to take my vacation until the fall. We're going to ... *(Gives up.)* Yes, if you feel it's ... Yes, I'll start my vacation tomorrow. Is that for three weeks or ... or is it longer? *(A short beat.)* Let me know. Please. Thank you. I do apologize for any embarrassment I might have caused ... you guys. *(He hangs up.)*

JESSIE. Did he fire you?

MORTON. He suggested we talk after my vacation.

JESSIE. *(Rises.)* We can't go to Sicily in the summer. It's too hot.

MORTON. I can't believe any of this.

JESSIE. We have to fight back. We need a plan. We have to have a plan. Is Harold the best man to represent you?

MORTON. No. I should get another lawyer. We could use Harold as a character witness if it becomes necessary. *(Paces anxiously; mops brow.)*

JESSIE. What about the psychiatric report?

MORTON. I have an appointment Friday with a Doctor Conners. I'd like you to come with me.

JESSIE. I want to. Do you know anything about the girl you were supposed to have ... goosed?

MORTON. Her name is Claudia Troyanski. She's a highschool senior and lives somewhere in the neighborhood. Thinking back on it ... I do remember what she was wearing. She was leaning over on the bench, tying her shoelace, so all I got was a general impression of her. But ... She had on a white tank top cotton shirt and very, very tight khaki shorts. Her legs were bare; no socks. Long, thin, bare legs and her backside in those tight khaki shorts ... It was sticking up in the air ... her backside...

JESSIE. She sounds like a little bitch to me.

MORTON. *(Mops brow.)* It was provocative. Her ass must have been ten feet up in the air!

JESSIE. Tramps, that's all these young girls are today. They roam the streets looking for pickups. Thank God Dougie is safe at Harvard.

MORTON. I don't think she knew I was passing her, but her posture, the way she leaned over to tie her shoelace, in those tight khaki shorts, it was ... it was like an invitation.

JESSIE. But you didn't touch her.

MORTON. No, though my leg might have brushed by her.

JESSIE. Your leg touched her?

MORTON. It might have. I was walking quite close to her.

JESSIE. I thought you said you'd have to lean over to touch her.

MORTON. *(Equivocating.)* Yes, I ... Well ... I was walking at an angle ... it might have been possible ... *(The phone rings. Jessie looks to Morton.)* Please.

JESSIE. *(Picks up phone; into phone.)* Yes? *(A short beat.)* This is Morton Bloom's residence. Who's calling? *(A short beat; hand over mouthpiece.)* It's CBS television. They'd like you to appear on *Live At Five* tomorrow afternoon.

MORTON. They've heard ... ? *(Jessie nods. Morton fiercely shakes head.)* No. Tell them no.

JESSIE. *(Into phone.)* Mr. Bloom is not interested. He asks that you do not disturb his privacy again. Thank you! *(She hangs up.)* It'll be in the morning newspapers.

MORTON. I can't believe it.

JESSIE. The New York Post will have a field day.

MORTON. They might use it as a headline.

JESSIE. They wouldn't...

MORTON. *(Kneads handkerchief.)* They might. I can see it now. *Corporate Attorney Gooses High School Senior on Columbus Avenue.*

JESSIE. Don't even think it!

MORTON. I'm ruined, Jessie. There's no way I can salvage anything. My job, my reputation, my license to practise...

JESSIE. Shhh. Shhh. No one will do anything to hurt you. You have friends in this city. Powerful friends. Political connections. My father is still a very influential...

MORTON. *(Moves to phone.)* Your father! I'll phone your father.

JESSIE. Wait! Wait one second. Before you do that, you must tell me ... is it possible, without you consciously knowing it, that you touched her? Slightly?

MORTON. I don't think so. I don't. Let's say this is the bench. *(He pulls a wooden chair D.)* Let's say I was coming from this direction. *(Moves far L., D.)* I was walking up at an angle, from near the curbstone. I remember I was feeling happy, carefree. Dougie was at law school, you and I finally having the time to do all the things we wanted to ... Travel, Europe, Sicily ... *(Starts walking toward chair.)* For some reason I walked away from the curbstone, toward the benches. But before getting to the benches, I turned and walked parallel to the benches. *(He does so; but stops in confusion in front of the chair.)* I don't know exactly ... I don't remember ... how close I was to the girl ... *(Turns about as if looking for a clue.)* Whether my leg touched her or my arm or whether I was too far away from her unless I leaned over...

JESSIE. Wait. Wait. Let me be the girl.

MORTON. Claudia Troyanski?

JESSIE. Yes, I'll be ... Claudia Troyanski. You get back to where you were. I'll put my foot on the bench and pretend I'm tying my shoelace. *(She does so, foot on chair.)* Is this how she did it?

MORTON. No, no, it wasn't. *(As if suddenly remembering.)* Her foot wasn't on the bench. She was near the bench but her feet were on the ground and she was bending over, at the waist, tying

15

her shoelace.

JESSIE. *(She does so; both feet on the ground.)* Is this it?

MORTON. *(It's just not the same backside.)* Well ... not exactly. She was wearing tight khaki shorts and she had long bare legs and her backside was, way up, way, way, way up in the, the...

JESSIE. *(Turns on him; angrily.)* Well, I don't have khaki shorts! And my backside does not have to be way, way, way, way up in the air for the purpose of what we are doing! *(Turns around.)* Is this ... generally how it looked? *(Bends over.)*

MORTON. *(A long disappointed beat.)* Yes. Generally.

JESSIE. *(Stands upright.)* Then please go back to where you were, near the curbstone there, and pass me as you passed that...

MORTON. Claudia Troyanski.

JESSIE. *(With effort.)* Claudia Troyanski.

MORTON. Good idea. *(He moves to far L.)*

JESSIE. Are you ready?

MORTON. I'm ready.

JESSIE. Begin walking! *(Bends over. Acting it out, Morton walks toward her, humming, swinging his arms at his sides. In his stride, without missing a beat, without a change of expression, he gooses Jessie with a stiff finger and whistles shrilly simultaneously. Jessie jumps upright with a gasp, grabs her backside with both hands, turns forward with a horrified expression. Morton continues walking as if he's done nothing out of the ordinary, humming; he reaches the R. wall and turns to Jessie. He seems surprised at what he sees.)*

MORTON. What ... What's wrong?

JESSIE. You goosed me!

MORTON. I did what?

JESSIE. I said you goosed me! Aren't you aware of it?

MORTON. No. It must have been my leg as I was passing...

JESSIE. It wasn't your leg! It was your finger! You took your finger and you stuck it ... you ... you ... *(Jabs her finger into the air.)* ... you did it! You did it right here in this room!

MORTON. That's odd. I have no recollection ... *(The phone rings. Jessie snaps at it.)*

JESSIE. *(Into phone.)* Yes! *(Apologetically.)* I'm sorry. Forgive me,

16

Dad. So much has been ... You heard? I don't know what to ... *(Sniffling.)* I will. Yes. I'll try. One second. *(Holds out phone to Morton.)* It's my father.

MORTON. *(Into phone.)* Judge, I'm glad you called. *(A short beat.)* It's been a nightmare. None of it makes sense to me. *(A short beat.)* I'm seeing a psychiatrist Friday. No, I haven't been overworking. It's not a nervous breakdown. It's ... It's all a horrible mistake! *(He glances at Jessie's grim face.)* Whatever you do, I'd certainly appreciate it. My love to mother. *(He hangs up.)* What were you...

JESSIE. Let's do it again, Morton. Please go back to where the curbstone would be and pass me up here.

MORTON. I'll pay attention this time. *(He moves far L.)*

JESSIE. Are you ready?

MORTON. I'm ready.

JESSIE. Begin! *(And she bends over. We now see an exact replay of what happened previously. Only this time Jessie starts shouting as soon as she turns forward, her hands clasped to her backside.)* There! There! You did it again! You did it again! *(Morton slowly turns to her.)* Don't you dare tell me you don't know what just happened!

MORTON. I goosed you?

JESSIE. Yes, you did.

MORTON. *(A short thoughtful beat.)* I ... I felt it this time.

JESSIE. You felt you goosed me?

MORTON. *(Nods; sits wearily in armchair.)* It's all so strange. It was like ... my body didn't seem to be part of me; it seemed to be moving of its own accord.

JESSIE. And the girl? Claudia Troyanski? Did you...?

MORTON. I don't remember. I have no recollection.

JESSIE. Think! Think! You must remember! We must know the truth so we can devise a plan to defend ourselves. Otherwise we will be ruined. They will destroy us!

MORTON. *(A short beat to pull himself together.)* I walked home from the office, as I do every day, up Fifty-seventh Street, across the Circle into Columbus Avenue. It had been an exceptionally good day for me. Harold and I had settled a two million dollar law-

17

suit and Whitmore...

JESSIE. Morton ... do you have to repeat it all? Can't you jump to when you first saw Claudia Troyanski?

MORTON. *(Jumps up; screams shrilly, hysterically.)* No, I can't, I can't! I'm not a machine! I'm not a computer! I am trying my best to recollect everything!

JESSIE. I'm sorry, I'm sorry. Forgive me. Anyway you want. Do it anyway you want. I won't interrupt again.

MORTON. *(Sits in armchair; starts speaking slowly; pleased.)* ... congratulated us; he said there had been some talk of our becoming full partners. You can imagine how happy that made me. I was feeling wonderful. I stopped off on Sixty-third Street and bought a tofutti ice cream cone. It was the first I ever had. It was delicious. Further on ... Ah! I know what it was! I know what I forgot!

JESSIE. What? What did you forget?

MORTON. *(Rises; paces; with new energy.)* As I moved up Columbus Avenue, I had this thought. I don't know where it came from. It just popped into my head. I thought: what would I do if I knew I had only one hour to live? how would I behave? how would I fill the time that was left to me? The idea wasn't depressing. I rather enjoyed thinking about it. The possibility of my demise wove itself in and out of my day dreaming about our trip to Sicily this fall. It occurred to me that if I had one hour left to live I still had a multitude of choices open to me. The ballgame wasn't over yet. I had one hour to live and within that time I could do anything I wanted; anything!

JESSIE. And that's when you saw her.

MORTON. Yes.

JESSIE. Tying her shoelace.

MORTON. On the museum side of Columbus Avenue.

JESSIE. You moved toward her.

MORTON. Yes.

JESSIE. Knowing that you had only one hour to live ... *(She stares at Morton, waiting for him to speak. He doesn't. He turns away from her, paces.)* You didn't run home to be with me. You didn't run to the nearest phone to talk to your son. You walked up to the bench

18

and you goosed Claudia Troyanski, a high school senior in tight khaki shorts. That was the choice you made. Of the multitude of choices. That was the choice you made. *(She sits on sofa; her hands clasped in her lap; her face without expression.)*

MORTON. *(Turns to her; seemingly overwhelmed by a new thought.)* I know what our plan is, Jessie! I know how we can beat them. You were right. Once I acknowledged to myself what really happened, everything fell into place. This is our plan. I've been working too hard. Exhaustion. Mental fatigue. I can get a stack of affidavits to substantiate that, call witnesses if need be. It's not going to be a problem. We've been blowing this way out of proportion. Your father and Mr. Whitmore can keep the media in check, threaten them with a lawsuit if they deviate one inch from the truth. And no court is going to do more than slap me on the wrist. My record is flawless. My reputation speaks for itself. What a relief! What a relief this is! I feel like a new man. Absolutely like a new man. *(He whistles, sits in armchair; shortly.)* What time do you suggest we go to dinner? *(Jessie doesn't reply.)* I'm looking forward to those chichimongas at Caramba's. *(Jessie doesn't reply.)* I think I'll have a vodka martini instead of a margarita, though. Cold and dry. *(Whistles; taps fingers.)* No need to hurry. We have all evening. Might as well enjoy it. *(Whistles; taps fingers.)* Whenever you say the word, we'll go. I am getting hungry. But it's entirely up to you, dear. It's entirely up to you. *(Whistles; taps fingers. Lights fade to black.)*

****

PROPERTY LIST

ONSTAGE
Telephone
Sofa
Magazine
Mail
Armchair
Handkerchief
Wooden chair

OFFSTAGE
Briefcase (Morton)

HOW WE REACHED AN IMPASSE ON NUCLEAR ENERGY

HOW WE REACHED AN IMPASSE ON NUCLEAR ENERGY

SCENE: The livingroom of the Wilson household in a Washington D.C. luxury co-op. Entrance door, Left, Downstage. A swinging door to the kitchen, rear, Left. A window in the rear wall. A door to the bedroom in rear wall, Right. A door to the bathroom in the Right wall.

TIME: Spring: late day.

AT RISE: The entrance door is opened with a key and Dennis Wilson enters. He is in a business suit, hat; carries a large suitcase and a briefcase.

DENNIS. *(Calls out.)* Rosalind? Rosalind? *(No answer. He moves into bedroom, closing door behind him. Rosalind exits from kitchen. She is carrying a dish with cheese on it. She is wearing a party dress, looks quite attractive; however, she has on her face a rather well groomed beard.)*

ROSALIND. *(Looks about.)* Dennis? Dennis? *(No answer. She returns to the kitchen. Dennis comes out of the bedroom without suitcase and briefcase.)*

DENNIS. Rosalind? *(And he enters the bathroom, closing the door behind him. Rosalind comes back into living room from kitchen. She is carrying a tray with hor d'oeuvres on it.)*

ROSALIND. *(Looks about.)* Dennis? *(She puts tray on coffee table in front of sofa and returns to kitchen. Dennis comes out of the bathroom, whistling a favorite aria. He is wiping his hands. When he is done, he tosses the towel into the bathroom and closes the bathroom door. He moves to the portable bar D.R. Still whistling, he pours himself a scotch, splashes soda from a siphon into the glass. He is about to drink when Rosalind enters from the kitchen, carrying a small tray with glasses on it.)* Dennis, I thought I heard you come in! *(She puts tray on side table, L. Dennis's back stiffens, his eyes widen. He removes his hat. Is that a beard on his wife's face? Rosalind moves to him with open arms.)* Is it you? Are you finally home? It's been a month, a whole month! Oh, darling, that's the longest we've ever been apart. Promise me you won't ever, ever leave me again. Promise. Promise. Promise. *(And she hugs him tightly. Dennis is dumbfounded. Is it a joke? Is it really a beard on her face?)*

DENNIS. *(Steps back.)* Rosalind ... what ... what is that ... *(Forces a laugh.)* It's funny. It is funny. Where in the world did you get it?

ROSALIND. Get what, sweetheart.

DENNIS. The ... beard.

ROSALIND. Oh, how stupid of me. I completely forgot. *(Strokes beard.)* I grew it while you were away.

DENNIS. *(A short puzzled beat.)* You grew it?

ROSALIND. Why are you surprised? You knew I shaved. I made no secret of it.

DENNIS. Yes, but...

ROSALIND. But what? *(She pours herself a scotch, splashes soda from siphon into glass.)*

DENNIS. I ... I was under the impression that you shaved only your legs and ... your armpits.

ROSALIND. What about my mustache?

DENNIS. Your mustache?

ROSALIND. Why are you repeating everything I say, sweetheart? You know I have a mustache.

DENNIS. Oh, not really. It's merely the faintest shadow of a mustache. I never took it seriously.

ROSALIND. Nonetheless it was there and I had to shave it.

DENNIS. Don't they have depilatory creams for that?

ROSALIND. Unfortunately I'm allergic to them, and I've always felt that electrolysis was a barbaric practice. *(Obviously disappointed.)* I take it you don't like the beard.

DENNIS. Like it?

ROSALIND. Dennis!

DENNIS. I'm sorry, dear. I've been flying for the last fifteen hours and I haven't turned around as yet. *(Gets another drink, splashes soda into glass.)* Is it ... a genuine beard?

ROSALIND. Darling, I told you...!

DENNIS. Just asking. I'm just asking. Frankly I don't understand why you ... want it. It does nothing for your appearance.

ROSALIND. *(A short sad beat.)* You're the first one to say that.

DENNIS. I am?

ROSALIND. Everyone else has complimented me on it.

DENNIS. They have?

ROSALIND. Perhaps you should think of going into analysis.

DENNIS. Don't, Rosalind; don't do that to me. Whenever we disagree you invariably suggest I go into analysis. Disagreeing with you doesn't *ipso facto* mean I need a shrink.

ROSALIND. But it's obvious you have a problem.

DENNIS. Which is?

ROSALIND. You refuse to acknowledge that females have male characteristics and males have female characteristics.

DENNIS. Is that what you think?

ROSALIND. Yes, that is what I think.

DENNIS. I refuse to acknowledge that there are male characteristics in the female.

ROSALIND. And *vice versa*.

DENNIS. That's a terrible thing to accuse me of, Rosalind.

ROSALIND. Do you prefer tact to honesty?

DENNIS. No, of course not. But your accusation is ludicrous. I have consistently acknowledged the intrinsic bisexuality of human beings. Let's not get off the track, however. I take it you don't believe a man has reason to be unhappy when on returning home from a month's trip abroad he finds that his wife has grown a beard.

ROSALIND. Not if that man opened his eyes and saw that during his absence many, many women have grown beards and that it has become quite fashionable.

DENNIS. I assure you my eyes have been open and I equally assure you that I have not seen a single woman with a beard!

ROSALIND. Perhaps you haven't looked in the right places. Betty Friedan has a beard; Gloria Steinem has a beard; Germaine Greer has a beard; Susan Brownmiller has a beard; and Goldie Hawn has a beard.

DENNIS. Fine. I stand corrected. But for the life of me I still don't understand why *you* want to have a beard if it doesn't make you look more attractive.

ROSALIND. *(Gets another drink, going through the same motions.)* Some might take exception to that remark. But that is not why we have beards, Mr. Wilson.

DENNIS. Ah, Mr. Wilson!

ROSALIND. We have beards because we no longer see the need to hide that part of ourselves which can be described as a male characteristic.

DENNIS. Does that mean you've also stopped shaving your legs and your ... armpits?

ROSALIND. Yes, it does.

DENNIS. Damn. This is turning out to be an extraordinary homecoming; extraordinary.

ROSALIND. I confess I am surprised at your reaction. I had somehow hoped that you would understand, that you would have said to me, "Sweetheart, if that's your choice, I respect it. I didn't marry a pretty face and a pair of boobs. I married a woman of independence and intelligence." But you can't say that to me, can you?

DENNIS. *(A short beat.)* No, I can't. I won't lie to you, Roz. I don't like it. It's a turn-off for me. *(Covers his eyes for a few beats.)* For God's sake, do you expect me to go on kissing you and cuddling you, and to dance cheek-to-cheek with you?

ROSALIND. If you had a beard, wouldn't I?

DENNIS. It's not the same.

ROSALIND. It is the same!

DENNIS. It ... *(Changes his mind.)* Rosalind, historically men have

26

grown beards and historically men look well in beards.

ROSALIND. And women don't?

DENNIS. No, they don't, and that's a fact! *(He gets another drink, going through the same motions.)*

ROSALIND. Nonsense. Sheer and utter nonsense. It's because you're not used to seeing women with beards, but once it becomes a common practice...

DENNIS. It'll never become a common practice. Men will never allow ... *(He bites his tongue, so to speak.)*

ROSALIND. *(Deadly stare.)* Never allow *what?*

DENNIS. *(Embarrassed.)* I ... I ... I apologize, Roasalind. I didn't mean that. You're your own person, second to none. Full and unqualified equality between the sexes has been my credo since puberty, and you know it.

ROSALIND. Thank you for the apology.

DENNIS. I take it you have no intention of shaving it off. *(No answer from Rosalind.)* Even if I ask you. *(No answer from Rosalind.)* Even if I said that no matter how much I love you I couldn't live with you so long as there was a beard on your face.

ROSALIND. Before I answer, let me say this: until today I've been very, very happy. I've been feeling absolutely wonderful about myself. For the first time since I don't know how long I felt all of a piece. I could finally look reality straight in the eye and say, "This is what I am. A woman. A man. A self-evident entity. A person."

DENNIS. Please don't try to fill me with guilt, Rosalind.

ROSALIND. Let me...

DENNIS. You're always doing that. Invariably it's my fault. I'm the culprit. Invariably your next suggestion is that I go into analysis.

ROSALIND. Let me finish, please. *(Gets another drink, going through the same motions.)* We're not children. We both know that this is our last chance to have a marriage and a life shared with someone else.

DENNIS. It *is* our last chance.

ROSALIND. I come from one long bad marriage and you come from two short bad marriages.

DENNIS. Our children paid heavily for our mistakes.

ROSALIND. Six months here, six months there...

DENNIS. Your three, my two ... I miss them all.

ROSALIND. If our marriage fails, what can we look forward to?

DENNIS. I'll never marry again; never.

ROSALIND. Nor I. After my divorce from Martin, I swore that that was it. I had enough. But when I met you ... Dennis, ask me why I fell in love with you.

DENNIS. *(A short beat.)* It's too sad. I can't.

ROSALIND. Please.

DENNIS. *(Takes a breath.)* Why ... Why ... *(Shakes his head.)* I can't.

ROSALIND. I fell in love with you because I thought you were a very, very special person. You behaved towards women with absolute fairness. There was no role playing in your nature, no conventional male prejudices and posturing. When I prepared dinner for you in my apartment, you went into the kitchen and you did the dishes and pots: no qualms, no display of sacrifice or generosity. You didn't hesitate to pick up the broom, take out the garbage, shop for food or soak my stockings if you thought my stockings needed soaking. More than the color of your eyes or the symmetry of your torso, I fell in love with you, Dennis, for being a woman's man as well as a man's man.

DENNIS. Intellectually I can applaud what you're doing. Emotionally ... *(A short beat.)* I'm sorry.

ROSALIND. You seemed to me to be so gentle, so sensitive; you weren't ashamed of your female qualities; you expressed them freely, and I loved you for it.

DENNIS. Don't misconstrue my position, Rosalind. I'm not ashamed of my womanhood.

ROSALIND. I know you're not. That's why all this is so absurd.

DENNIS. *(Gets another drink, going through the same motions.)* It's one thing to express the opposite sex inside oneself; it's another to

28

physicalize it.

ROSALIND. But I've seen you physicalize the female in you.

DENNIS. When have you ever seen me...

ROSALIND. Many, many times. Don't you enjoy opening my perfume bottles and sniffing at them?

DENNIS. Oh, that.

ROSALIND. How about when you look through my jewelry box and casually put on a necklace or a bracelet?

DENNIS. For fun. That's merely for fun!

ROSALIND. Do you remember the night you came home drunk from a party at the Belskys?

DENNIS. *(Thinking.)* Uhhh...

ROSALIND. Do you remember what you did?

DENNIS. *(Thinking.)* Uhhh ... *(Abruptly.)* No.

ROSALIND. You put on my bra and panties.

DENNIS. *(Thinking.)* Uhhh...

ROSALIND. And you pranced around the room as if you were Queen of the May. I rarely saw you as happy as you were that night.

DENNIS. Ah! I remember now. I was quite drunk and I had no idea what I was doing.

ROSALIND. Can we try an experiment, Dennis?

DENNIS. *(Suspiciously.)* What kind of experiment?

ROSALIND. Sit down here. Close your eyes and don't move. *(She leads him to armchair; he sits.)* Trust me. I'm not going to hurt you and I'm not going to take advantage of your trust. This is an experiment. I want to see if there's any hope for saving our marriage. To fail again. To fail finally. To know there's nothing ahead for either one of us. I don't want it to happen. I don't. *(She takes out one of her wigs from a drawer; she puts it on Dennis's head.)* When all is said and done, Dennis, I truly thought that our marriage would be forever. Secretly I felt that we had been made for each other. It would be horrible if our children were told that we failed again. My Martin remarried happily; your Kate and Maryann remarried happily. We *can't* let this happen to us. We have to fight for our marriage and our love. *(She takes out makeup kit, puts a vivid red lipstick on Dennis's mouth and a moon of white powder on each of his cheeks.)* All I ask is that you be fair, Dennis; that you don't carry over any prejudices out of habit or laziness. I know in my heart of hearts that you and I share many personal fantasies and have innumerable emotional similarities. I know in my heart of hearts that you are going to like yourself more now than you ever have before. *(She holds up a hand mirror.)* Open your eyes, dear. *(Dennis opens his eyes and stares at his reflection. He takes hand mirror from her, tilts and turns his head every which way, blinking his eyes, licking his red lips, primping his wig, etc. He is trying to decide whether or not he likes his new appearance. Rosalind speaks shortly.)* What do you think?

DENNIS. I like it.

ROSALIND. Are you comfortable with how you look?

DENNIS. Surprisingly comfortable.

ROSALIND. You don't feel foolish, do you?

DENNIS. Surprisingly not.

ROSALIND. You don't feel physicalizing your female characteristics demeaning, do you?

DENNIS. Surprisingly not.

ROSALIND. There's a naturalness about your appearance now.

DENNIS. Yes, there is. I like myself. I do like myself.

ROSALIND. What a relief that is to me. Let's not talk about it for a while, dearest. Let's get on with our lives and enjoy your being home. May I get you a drink?

DENNIS. *(Hands her empty glass.)* Please. *(Returns to stare at his reflection in hand mirror.)*

ROSALIND. *(Pours drinks, going through the same motions as previously.)* How was Moscow?

DENNIS. Good. Good. A little chilly, but good. *(Crosses leg.)*

ROSALIND. Were the people any happier than when we were there last summer?

DENNIS. Oh, yes. I saw quite a number of them chuckling.

ROSALIND. Chuckling. How nice.

DENNIS. Once, in a gypsy restaurant, I saw a group of agricultural students double-over with laughter. Spontaneously. *(He primps his wig.)*

30

ROSALIND. They say there's going to be more progress on disarmament.

DENNIS. That's definitely under consideration.

ROSALIND. Then your trip was a success?

DENNIS. Definitely a success. They had us visit over twenty of their nuclear plants. The safety measures they've taken since Chernobyl are impressive, *very* impressive. *(He puts aside hand mirror, picks up a nail file from side table and files his nails.)*

ROSALIND. You're confident there won't be another nuclear accident?

DENNIS. Oh, yes.

ROSALIND. Anywhere in the world?

DENNIS. Oh, yes. Exceedingly confident. As Commissioner of the Nuclear Power Agency, I couldn't live with myself if I had any doubts about it.

ROSALIND. *(She puts his drink on side table near him; sits on sofa.)* After all, you are the father of young children.

DENNIS. I'm well aware of it. My children, your children, the children of the world are enormously affected by the decisions of our Agency.

ROSALIND. It's comforting to hear you say that, but ... You know, darling, there were serious nuclear accidents before Chernobyl. In Canada, the United States, Japan, England...

DENNIS. Of course I know it. It's my business to know it.

ROSALIND. Sweetheart, don't be angry with me. I've been having terrible nightmares lately.

DENNIS. You have? I am sorry. What about?

ROSALIND. The possibility of another nuclear accident.

DENNIS. *(Disappointedly.)* Rosalind...

ROSALIND. I can't help it. Last week I joined the Anti-Nuclear Association For A Cleaner World. I'm an Assistant Treasurer.

DENNIS. You should have spoken to me about it first.

ROSALIND. I know I should have. But so much is at stake. The future of the...

DENNIS. I'm well aware of that too. I'm not without maternal instinct.

31

ROSALIND. I know you're not. And I love you for it.

DENNIS. What you don't understand is that everything is under control. We're not idiots. This is our field of expertise. We all learned from the disaster at Chernobyl. It just won't ever happen again.

ROSALIND. I don't want us to quarrel, sweetheart, but ... You can't say that with absolute certainty.

DENNIS. No one can say *anything* with absolute certainty!

ROSALIND. Then why go on building nuclear plants that can destroy us all if we're *not* absolutely certain.

DENNIS. Rosalind, there isn't a country in the world that isn't building or planning to build nuclear plants. We need them to generate our technology. Natural resources are limited. Nuclear power is unlimited. It's as simple as that.

ROSALIND. What is simple about filling the atmosphere with deadly radioactive particles. What is simple about making uninhabitable vast areas of the earth?

DENNIS. *(Jumps to his feet.)* I already told you it was under control. Why don't you listen...

ROSALIND. *(Jumps to her feet.)* You have to resign from the Agency, Dennis. I won't allow you to be part of ... of that murderous bunch any longer!

DENNIS. *(Gets another drink, splashes soda into glass.)* You won't allow me! *You* won't allow me! What is wrong with you this evening, Rosalind? Why are you pushing me, pushing me, pushing me!

ROSALIND. I'm not. I'm just...

DENNIS. Frankly I find your behavior offensive. The more I give you, the more you want.

ROSALIND. That's not true.

DENNIS. It's not enough I give up my cultural and biological prerogatives; it's not enough I compromise my male identity by physicalizing my secondary female characteristics! Now I have to give up being Commissioner of the Nuclear Power Agency as well!

ROSALIND. *(Gets another drink, splashes soda into glass.)* I am talking about the future, Dennis! The future of our children, the future of ourselves, the future of the whole planet!

DENNIS. No, you're not. You're talking about how much more you can get out of me!

ROSALIND. *(Disappointedly.)* Dennis...

DENNIS. Don't think I don't know the game you're playing! It's not going to work. On this I intend to be firm. You're not going to strip me entirely of the last vestiges of my manhood!

ROSALIND. Your manhood?

DENNIS. Yes, damn it! You won't be happy until I'm a mere shadow of you, a disposable appendage to your obsessive lust for dominance! *(Gets another drink, no soda this time.)*

ROSALIND. That's absurd. What lust for dominance?

DENNIS. I'm on to you! I'm on to you!

ROSALIND. Do you think that's why I'm against nuclear power? To dominate? To win some childish game?

DENNIS. It's there. It's in the picture. You're not fooling anyone.

ROSALIND. Dennis, we're in danger; in mortal danger. This madness has to stop. It has nothing to do with us, with our relationship; it has to do with the continued existence of our species.

DENNIS. So you would have me believe. But unfortunately I don't believe it. It took me years to get appointed Commissioner of the Nuclear Power Agency. Years! Now you would strip me of my commission despite all the evidence that has been accumulated to prove the safety of nuclear energy. Oh, no, lady. Oh, no. Enough! That's enough stripping! Enough hacking! Enough castrating! Enough! Enough! *(Gets another drink, no soda this time.)*

ROSALIND. Dennis, you're acting irrationally!

DENNIS. *(With passion but not out of control.)* Irrationally? Is your next line that I should go into analysis?

ROSALIND. Perhaps, you ... *(Drops it.)* No, not at all. But why can't we talk?

DENNIS. *(Pacing.)* Because you don't want to convince me of the dangers of nuclear power. That's not it. You want me beaten,

33

vanquished, subdued to passivity!

ROSALIND. That isn't true. I do want to convince you that what I'm saying is the only hope we have: an end to nuclear power, of every kind. That's all I want. That's all I'm interested in. I have material here from the association ... *(She takes out a stack of pamphlets from the side table drawer.)*

DENNIS. Oh, I have your number, Rosalind nee Strasberg! This is what you've been after from the first day we met! Love me? Oh, no, not love me: destroy me!

ROSALIND. *(Eagerly.)* Listen. Listen to this. *(Reads quickly, parts of information from pamphlet.)* "There are over 375 commercial nuclear plants in operation ... A count of the accidents cannot be made with any accuracy since many governments conceal the occurrences of such accidents."

DENNIS. *(Pacing; hands on ears.)* I'm not listening! I have no intention of listening!

ROSALIND. *(Proceeds determinedly.)* "The United States has 101 commercial nuclear plants; France has 44; the Soviet Union has 51..."

DENNIS. Rave on! Rave on! It's of no consequence to me!

ROSALIND. "Britain has 35; West Germany 20; Canada 15..."

DENNIS. *(Removes hands from ears; still pacing.)* This is my final word, Rosalind nee Strasberg! Despite acknowledging my secondary female characteristics, I am still a man. I am still the Nuclear Power Commissioner. On this I will not budge. On this I will not give you an inch! I've gone far enough in my compromises; in giving into you; in deferring again and again to your insidious needs!

ROSALIND. *(Proceeds determinedly, quickly.)* "It's projected that a core meltdown at Shoreham stands to leave 40,000 early fatalities, 75,000 early injuries, 35,000 cancer deaths..."

DENNIS. I won't change anymore! I won't! I am still a man! I am still the Nuclear Power Commissioner!

ROSALIND. "...At the Indian Point 3 nuclear plant, early fatalities would be as high as 50,000, 167,000 early injuries, 14,000 cancer death, 314 billion dollars in property damage."

DENNIS. *(Facing front; stationary; eyes pinched tightly; fists clenched, face contorted with anguished resolve.)* I am still a man! I am still the Nuclear Power Commissioner! *(The stage darkens, gradually. Rosalind is lost in darkness. A spotlight pinpoints Dennis's bawling face in a yellowish glare.)*

ROSALIND. "For the Salem 2 nuclear plant, the estimate is 100,000 early fatalities, 75,000 early injuries, 14,000..."

DENNIS. I am still a man! I am still the Nuclear Power Commissioner!

ROSALIND. "Dr. Richard Webb argues that the Sandia report did not consider a massive reactor explosion."

DENNIS. I am still a man! I am still the Nuclear Power Commissioner!

ROSALIND. *(Reads very quickly.)* "He said that in terms of the deaths ... from the plume of radioactivity in a severe nuclear plant accident..."

DENNIS. *(Increasing anguish; tearing the words from deep inside himself.)* I am still a man! I am still the Nuclear Power Commissioner!

ROSALIND. "He said that if the plume moved on New York City, the number of deaths could be close to a million."

DENNIS. I am still a man! I am still the Nuclear Power Commissioner!

ROSALIND. "Up to 100,000 square miles of land could face abandonment in the wake of a serious nuclear plant accident."

DENNIS. I am still a man! I am still the Nuclear Power Commissioner!

ROSALIND. "Just prior to the Chernobyl nuclear accident, the Russian minister of power and electricity, was asked how safe the nuclear plants in Russia were. He answered, 'The odds of a meltdown are one in 10,000 years."

DENNIS. I am still a man! I am still the Nuclear Power Commissioner!" *(Voice and light fades.)* I am still a man! I am still the Nuclear Power Commissioner! I am still a man! I am still the Nuclear Power Commissioner .. *(Blackout.)*

PROPERTY LIST

ONSTAGE
Coffee table
Sofa
Portable bar
Side table
Wig
Makeup kit
Hand mirror
Nail file
Stack of pamphlets

OFFSTAGE
Large suitcase and briefcase (Dennis)
Dish (with cheese) (Rosalind)
Tray (with hor d'oeuvres) (Rosalind)
Towel (Dennis)
Small tray (with glasses) (Rosalind)

74 GEORGIA AVENUE

74 GEORGIA AVENUE

SCENE: The kitchen: an enamel-topped table and three wooden chairs, Center, Upstage; two windows with faded, diaphanous curtains in rear wall; Right wall. Downstage, foyer, leading to bedrooms, and Upstage, a sink and a bathroom door; Left wall, Downstage, entrance door, and Upstage, an old refrigerator, gas range, cabinets on Right and Left walls. Almost everything is chipped, aged, tarnished; the floorboards are covered with layers of ancient linoleum. Still the place is immaculately clean, functionally simple, without any decoration or extraneous piece.

TIME: Early evening: the last flush of sunlight.

AT RISE: Joseph Watson, a black man, is seated Downstage, Left, at table, turning the pages of The New York Post, slowly, indifferently, his mind elsewhere. There is a flat, vibrationless doorbell ring. Joseph, whose back is to the entrance door, stares across the room as if trying to guess who is at the door. The doorbell rings again.

JOSEPH. *(Without turning; dully.)* It's open. *(Marty Robbins enters. He is about ten years older than Joseph. He carries a very expensive suitcase. He is flawlessly dressed and preened, every hair in place, a picture of self-made elegance.)*
MARTY. *(Looking about; with astonishment.)* It's the same. It's practically the same. The cabinets, the sink, the floor ... *(Joseph turns in his chair. On seeing that his visitor is white, he immediately falls into an exaggerated street patois, playing the ghetto clown, convincingly.)*

JOSEPH. *(Jumps to his feet; wide-eyed.)* What you doin' in here? Who let you in?

MARTY. You...

JOSEPH. Anybody see you come up here? Anybody on the street? *(He hurries to window, R., leans against wall, peeks out, like a movie gangster, so he can't be seen from the street.)*

MARTY. No, I...

JOSEPH. How you get in this neighborhood? You got a car downstairs?

MARTY. A cab dropped me...

JOSEPH. Where you get the cab?

MARTY. Manhattan.

JOSEPH. *(Without moving from wall, he pulls down window shade.)* You live in Manhattan?

MARTY. Yes.

JOSEPH. Where?

MARTY. Central Park West, I'm...

JOSEPH. Shhh! Shhh! *(He crawls under windowsill to lean against wall near second window; peeks out as previously.)*

MARTY. Can you tell me what the mystery's about?

JOSEPH. *(Arm outstretched, he pulls down second window shade.)* You know where you is or you been smokin' grass?

MARTY. I'm at 74 Georgia Avenue, the East New York section of Brooklyn.

JOSEPH. Then you should know that they don't even let white policemen walk in this neighborhood, honkey. By comin' into my house you have jeopardized my reputation an' my physical well bein'.

MARTY. But no one saw me come in. I'm positive. Let me introduce myself. I'm Martin Robbins. You can call me Marty. *(Extends hand.)*

JOSEPH. *(Looks at his hand, distrustfully, looks around the room, then grabs Marty's hand, pumps it once; drops it.)* Joseph Watson. You can call me Mr. Watson.

MARTY. Glad to meet you, Mr. Watson.

JOSEPH. The same here, Martin.

MARTY. You know, I was born in this apartment.

JOSEPH. You was born in this apartment?

MARTY. My room was the second one in the foyer, overlooking the alley.

JOSEPH. *(With greater emphasis.)* You was born right here in this apartment?

MARTY. Yes, I was. I know every inch of this place.

JOSEPH. Well, I'll be a stack of potato latkes.

MARTY. What did you say?

JOSEPH. I didn't say nothin', Martin.

MARTY. I was nineteen when I moved out. I haven't been back until now. But I've been ... Look! Look at this! It's still here! Wow, this is amazing! *(He moves to door frame; examines it.)* Every year I used to mark my height with a notch on this board. *(He measures his height with the flat of his hand, standing against the door frame.)* It was a ritual with me. I could, like, watch myself grow every ... *(He steps back, looks at where his hand marked his present height.)* Whatta you know. I shrunk three inches since I was nineteen.

JOSEPH. So you lived in the same apartment I'm livin' in now.

MARTY. The exact same apartment.

JOSEPH. Well, I'll be a bowl of karsha varnishkes.

MARTY. What's that?

JOSEPH. Nothin', man. I'm jus' jawbonin'.

MARTY. Of course almost the whole neighborhood was white when I lived here.

JOSEPH. I know that from the cockroaches you left behind.

MARTY. You forgot it was still a very poor neighborhood then. Uhhh, do you mind if I sit down?

JOSEPH. *(Not wanting him to stay.)* Where?

MARTY. In one of those chairs at the table.

JOSEPH. Those chairs?

MARTY. Is there something wrong with those chairs?

JOSEPH. Nothin' wrong wit' 'em except they're taken.

MARTY. How can they be taken? No one's sitting in them.

JOSEPH. No one's sittin' in 'em this minute. But that's not to say nobody's gonna be sittin' in 'em in the near future!

MARTY. *(Moves about, touching, looking.)* It doesn't matter. You wouldn't believe how excited I am. I've been thinking of coming here for years. My grandfather owned this house. He lived on the first floor and we lived up here. What was unusual is that my grandfather had ten children, seven girls and three boys, and all of them, after they married and had kids, all of them lived in the neighborhood, within a half dozen blocks of this place. We were really a close family. I mean, on weekends and holidays this place was filled to the rafters with relatives and friends and friends of friends and ... It was like a fantastic party all the time, with everyone eating and drinking and talking and cracking jokes ... Not that there wasn't fights in the family. My God, did we have fights! I don't think there were two days in a row when everyone was talking to everyone else. There was always this one not talking to that one, and that one mad at the other one, and ... *(Suddenly stops.)* I'm sorry. I got carried away.

JOSEPH. *(Sits at table; U.C.)* You sure did. Any chance you gettin' carried away out of these premises?

MARTY. *(Sits D.R., table.)* That's what I want to discuss with you ... Mr. Watson. You have to know I had no idea who'd be living here...

JOSEPH. No reason you should. This area has undergone some radical transformations since you been around.

MARTY. Unbelievable. It looks like Hiroshima must have looked after they dropped the atom bomb. There are more burned-out buildings and empty lots and ... Up front I don't expect you to do anything for nothing.

JOSEPH. You expect correctly.

MARTY. I'm willing to pay.

JOSEPH. Then I'm willing to listen.

MARTY. I'd like to move in.

JOSEPH. Where?

MARTY. Here.

JOSEPH. Here?

MARTY. Yes. I brought enough clothes for a week.

42

JOSEPH. How long?

MARTY. A week. But I may want to stay longer.

JOSEPH. *(Glances at Marty's suitcase.)* You puttin' me on.

MARTY. No. I'm serious. I'll pay you fifty dollars for every night I stay here.

JOSEPH. *(Rises; feigned indignation.)* Where do you get your nerve? You come into my home, you jeopardize my reputation, in my neighborhood, and you have the effrontery — if that is the word in this situation — you have the effrontery to *assuuume* that this is some kind of cheap boarding house where I rent out rooms for dirty! filthy! lucre! *(There is the sound of someone wagging a tiny bell in offstage bedroom. Suddenly grim; in normal voice.)* See what you made me do. I woke her up.

MARTY. Who?

JOSEPH. My wife, that's who! *(He removes pitcher of iced water from refrigerator.)*

MARTY. She was sleeping? At this hour?

JOSEPH. We go to bed early if it's any of your business. I want you out of here by the time I get back. I'm done playing games with you. *(And he moves into the foyer, closing the first bedroom door, offstage, quietly behind him. Marty takes a bottle of cognac from his suitcase and places it on table. He then goes into bathroom, carrying suitcase with him. Joseph comes into kitchen. He spots the cognac at once. He looks around: Marty has left, he believes. He pours cognac into a glass and sits, U.C. He glances at newspaper, sips cognac. Marty comes out of bathroom. He has removed jacket and tie, opened shirt collar and wears cardigan sweater.)*

MARTY. *(Claps his hands.)* You're not getting ... *("Rid of me that easy" would have followed. Joseph jumps out of his chair, perhaps howls, playing it like an old movie Negro.)*

JOSEPH. You insane, man? *(Looks to front door; back to Marty.)* What you doin' hidin' in my bathroom an' scarin' the life outta me! I thought I told you I wanted you out of my house!

MARTY. I can't leave. Not yet. Please. How much do you want? Tell me. Give me a figure.

JOSEPH. *(Sits down; mumbles.)* I ain't for sale, *Mr.* Robbins. No

43

amount of money will get you into this house.

MARTY. *(Sits at table.)* Look, if I insulted you, I apologize. I ... Can I stay tonight? One night. I'll leave in the morning, I promise.

JOSEPH. *(Mumbles; turning pages of newspaper.)* Why is stayin' so damn important to you?

MARTY. I don't really know. I have a great need to be here, in this apartment, where I was ... born and ... grew up ... *(A long beat.)* I didn't marry until I was forty-one. My wife's a good deal younger than I am. We have a two year old son. Lately my wife and I have been fighting a lot and ... I'm wiped out.

JOSEPH. *(Eyes on newspaper.)* I never heard of any Robbins family.

MARTY. Rabinowitz. It was Rabinowitz.

JOSEPH. Your Zada's name was Schapiro.

MARTY. Zada? How do you know...?

JOSEPH. *(Eyes still on newspaper.)* My father was janitor of your synagogue for a long time.

MARTY. You're kidding.

JOSEPH. He was janitor until they tore down the building. You were out of the neighborhood by then, like most of your relatives and friends. I got to know the old people who stayed behind. The Talmud Torah Or Chodesh.

MARTY. That's right! That's what it was called. I kept thinking of it as the Williams Avenue Synagogue. It was on Williams Avenue but it was called the Talmud Torah Or Chodesh. *(He gets another glass and pours cognac for himself and Joseph, sitting at table again.)* This is great. This is what I came here for. To talk to somebody who knows what it was like...

JOSEPH. *(Turns pages of newspaper.)* My father's name was Leon. He turned on the lights when you people weren't allowed to do it. Sometimes he'd stand in the back during services. To listen. Did you know him?

MARTY. I don't think so.

JOSEPH. I'd be with him sometime. When you were goin' to the synagogue I was only a kid. Do you remember seein' me there?

44

MARTY. I'm sorry. I don't recall seeing any black person there.

JOSEPH. *(Puts newspaper aside.)* We must have been the original invisible *schvartzes.* I suppose nobody saw us. *(He drinks.)*

MARTY. Where did you live when you were a kid?

JOSEPH. Snedeker Avenue.

MARTY. Did you go to P.S. 63?

JOSEPH. *(Nods.)* And from there to 173 and then to Thomas Jefferson High School.

MARTY. Me, too. Did you know Miss Brenner in 63?

JOSEPH. I had Miss Brenner! She was my homeroom teacher!

MARTY. Mine, too! Mine, too! Did you know Charlie Marello?

JOSEPH. His parents owned a grocery store on Atlantic Avenue?

MARTY. That's right. We went to school together. He was the toughest kid in the neighborhood. All he wanted was to become a gangster.

JOSEPH. He did.

MARTY. You're kidding me.

JOSEPH. Uhuh. He robbed the East New York Savings Bank on the corner and got twenty to life.

MARTY. How do you like that. He got what he wanted.

JOSEPH. You said it, man, I didn't! *(And they both break out in laughter. There is the sound of Joseph's wife ringing the tiny bell in her offstage bedroom. At once Joseph becomes grim. He rises.)* Excuse me. *(And he exits to bedroom. Marty fills glasses with cognac. He then rises and dials phone.)*

MARTY. *(Into phone.)* Berthel? Mr. Robbins. Is my wife in? Put her on, please. *(He swallows cognac.)* Hi. *(A short beat.)* What difference does it make where I go? *(A short beat.)* You care? Really? Who are you kidding? I don't think you cared from the first day you married me. *(A short Beat.)* Cry. Cry. Go ahead. That's an old technique of yours. You're not fooling anyone. I'm gonna tell you a secret, Cindy. You don't have any feelings for me. You give me zilch, absolute zilch. All you do is take. From the beginning ... *(He's interrupted.)* Don't bring David into this. David was an accident and you know it! *(Joseph enters, goes to cabinet and takes out medicine, moves back to bedroom, offstage, turning on kitchen light. Marty speaks with his hand over mouthpiece of phone; to Joseph.)* I took the liberty ... *(Joseph merely nods and exits. Marty speaks into phone.)* Stop with the crying already. All right. It wasn't an accident. You gave me David. All right. I believe you. *(A short beat.)* No, not that. What you say you feel for me, I don't feel it. I'm sorry. I don't. *(A short beat.)* I won't be home tonight. No. I don't know when I'll be home. I'll keep you informed. *(A short beat.)* I'd appreciate it if you didn't say anything to David. A business trip is fine. Thank you. *(He hangs up. Joseph comes in, returns medicine to cabinet. He then sits at table, downs drink in a single swallow.)* Is your wife sick? *(Joseph nods.)* Very sick?

JOSEPH. *(Nods. A beat.)* Soon I'll be moving out of this neighborhood myself. Won't be anything to keep me here.

MARTY. What do you do for a living?

JOSEPH. I was working as a computer operator for the Brooklyn Gas Company. But I gave it up. To see to her. To be ... *(A beat.)* What do you do?

MARTY. Years ago I started my own advertising agency with a friend. We sold it last August. I've been sort of bouncing around since then, looking to get into something new. *(A beat.)* You keep busy?

JOSEPH. I go out for groceries, the newspaper. I got books to read and ... I like to jus' sit here rememberin' the old men from the synagogue: Mr. Bushlevitz, Cantor Levinson, Mr. Ashkenazy...

MARTY. I haven't heard anyone mention those names in I don't know how long.

JOSEPH. After the synagogue was torn down I used to see them in the neighborhood. But mostly I saw them at funerals. How come you didn't go to your grandfather's funeral?

MARTY. *(Disingenuously.)* I ... I couldn't make it. I was in Los Angeles and ... I couldn't get back in time. My parents were there.

JOSEPH. I saw them. And your aunts and uncles and cousins ... It had to be the biggest funeral they ever had. *(Beckons Marty nearer to*

46

him.) I got his jacket, his skullcap and his cane.

MARTY. You got what?

JOSEPH. I got your grandfather's jacket, skullcap and cane.

MARTY. How did you get them?

JOSEPH. He left them in the synagogue. In the office. My father asked me to help him clean up and I kept the ... *(Suddendly rises; moves into foyer.)* You wait there. Don't go 'way. I'll show you. *(He re-enters kitchen almost at once from foyer, pulling in a portable coatrack on which a line of jackets, some with prayer shawls on them, are hanging in a row; on the bottom shelf there are several pairs of shoes, some with spats, galoshes and rubbers; on the top shelf are a number of hats and skullcaps of different sizes and shapes; also two cardboard boxes, one with prayer shawls, the other with prayer books; a two-foot mirror hangs from top of rack, at the side.)*

MARTY. *(Rises; examines clothes.)* I don't believe it. My God, this is fantastic. I can almost smell the synagogue from these clothes. What a collection! Did ... Did this belong to Mr. Bushlevitz? *(He removes a swallow-tailed tuxedo jacket from rack.)*

JOSEPH. That's his. You remember on holidays he used to wear a full-dress tuxedo with a ruffled shirt and bowtie? You'll find the bowtie in the right-hand pocket.

MARTY. Unbelievable. And this ... this is Cantor Levinson's. *(He removes a white satin cantorial robe from rack.)*

JOSEPH. *(Nods.)* When he used to sing, I'd get goose bumps all over. That man's voice was pure soul music.

MARTY. I don't get it ... Joseph. What are you saving these clothes for?

JOSEPH. They're part of *my* growing-up; part of *my* history. *(Stares at Marty for a beat.)*

MARTY. That makes two of us.

JOSEPH. Sometimes I put a jacket and a yarmulke on and ... they help me get through the night.

MARTY. How do they do that?

JOSEPH. They remind me of different ... people. Of my father. Of my wife before she ... Of the old Jews who prayed in the synagogue when I was a kid. I guess mostly they remind me of the old

Jews. I can hear them and see them and kind of be ... them.

MARTY. I don't understand.

JOSEPH. I don't either. But it makes me feel good not to be myself for a while and pray in a way I don't normally pray.

MARTY. You pray in Hebrew?

JOSEPH. *(Laughing.)* Don't ask me how I do it, man, but that's how it sounds to me. The words could be comin' from someplace in my memory or they could jus' be comin' from somebody else.

MARTY. I swear, you're beginning to sound spooky. Who's somebody else?

JOSEPH. Damn if I know. I'm jus' tryin' to tell you what I feel when I put on those clothes.

MARTY. Show me.

JOSEPH. You...?

MARTY. Yeah. Show me. Let me see what happens.

JOSEPH. I never did it for anybody before.

MARTY. There's always a first time.

JOSEPH. *(Hesitates.)* It is spooky. I don't know...

MARTY. Come on, man. Don't make such a big thing out of it.

JOSEPH. *(A short beat; looking about.)* I don't want to discuss it with you after I'm done. And I don't want you to repeat to anybody what it is I'm doin'.

MARTY. I swear. Mum's the word. Now let's see this great mysterious performance of yours. *(Joseph still hesitates, then nods abruptly. He puts on Mr. Bushlevitz's tuxedo jacket, clip-on bowtie, a prayer shawl, and a low, black, crown-shaped yarmulke.)*

JOSEPH. Anybody hear about this, I could be put in an institution.

MARTY. They could put us both in an institution. Don't forget, I'm the one who talked you into it. *(He sits in a chair, to watch. Joseph's body is now ramrod straight, his facial expression changes as he gradually turns into a semblance of Mr. Bushlevitz. He checks himself out in mirror hanging from rack. He clears his throat several times, clasps his hands behind his back, and speaks in a stern voice that is educated and without inflection.)*

48

JOSEPH/BUSHLEVITZ. Moishe, come over here. I have something to ask you. *(Marty doesn't move: he's hypnotized by Joseph's transformation.)* You should be ashamed of yourself. I watched you during services this morning and when they were saying Kaddish you stood up and said Kaddish too! For whom were you saying Kaddish, Moishe? Your father isn't dead! Your mother isn't dead! For who were you saying Kaddish? Could you be so stupid as to say Kaddish for a parent who isn't dead? What would your grandfather do if I told him this! Now where are you going? Moishe, Moishe, come back here! I am not finished with you! Moishe, come baaack heeere! *(He breathes heavily for several beats, then, grinning widely, speaks in his own voice.)* Well, what do you think about that?

MARTY. I ... I can't believe ... How ... How could you know I had that conversation with Mr. Bushlevitz?

JOSEPH. *(Returning Mr. Bushlevitz's clothes to rack.)* I told you I didn't want any discussion ... *(But now he's also anxious to talk about it.)* I don't know. Unless it's my memory, like I said. It could be I'm rememberin' something I overheard when I was a kid and it jus' comes out of me.

MARTY. *(Rises.)* That's impossible. I never saw you in the synagogue. If you had been anywhere near where I was I would have seen you.

JOSEPH. *(Gives up.)* You got me.

MARTY. Joe, did you ever hear of a dybbuk?

JOSEPH. A what?

MARTY. A dybbuk. There's a Jewish legend that the soul of a dead person can enter the body of a living person and control it for its own selfish reasons.

JOSEPH. You serious?

MARTY. It's a legend. I'm not saying it's true. But there were plays and books written about dybbuks and ... I'm not that familiar with it, but I think once he gets inside you he can make you do anything he wants.

JOSEPH. It can't be that. If I don't put these clothes on, nobody can make me do anything. And I can get back to myself by takin' those clothes off. It's gotta be my memory.

MARTY. Yeah. I guess so. You were probably around and I just don't remember seeing you.

JOSEPH. I don't want to discuss this anymore. *(He starts to move out with coatrack. Marty stops him.)*

MARTY. Why don't you let that go for now. Let's ... Let's have another drink. *(Leads him to table.)* Do you like the cognac? It cost me about forty bucks. I cut down my drinking when I sold the agency. Doctor's advice. You know, when you've been working all your life ... I'm talking fifteen, sixteen hours a day, seven days a week ... It's pretty damn hard to shut the motor. It's like you're still running but your legs aren't moving. Joe ... let me stay the night. Please.

JOSEPH. *(Shakes his head.)* It'll be to...

MARTY. My old room is empty, isn't it?

JOSEPH. It's empty. But you'll be up all night. My wife...

MARTY. I don't care about that. I'm not here to sleep. We can spend the night talking, drinking, having a few laughs. Why not?

JOSEPH. Why you so against going home?

MARTY. *(A short beat.)* There's nothing there for me.

JOSEPH. You have a lot of fights with your wife, huh?

MARTY. Constantly. She doesn't understand. She doesn't make the effort to understand. If she saw this neighborhood, where I came from, what I had to do to achieve what I achieved ... Nah. It wouldn't have made any difference. She's a kid. Everything was given to her with a silver spoon. They're trained to be takers, Joe. They take. That's the younger generation. They don't know how to give.

JOSEPH. What do you want her to give?

MARTY. Herself. Affection. Love. I want her to be generous with her emotions. I don't feel anything from her. She says all the right words and does the right things but ... It's not enough. For me it's not enough. I ... I don't believe her. *(A beat.)* What do you and your wife fight about? *(Joseph merely stares at him.)* I mean ... before she became sick.

50

JOSEPH. I guess what most married people fight about. But it was fun. *(Laughs.)* We had fun fighting. We'd poke and pick at one another and it'd end up huggin' and kissin' and ... *(A pained expression crosses his face.)* It's not the same for us. We don't fight. No more. What's peculiar about dyin' is that it doesn't bring you together. It tears you apart. It leaves you alone. With your own thoughts and your own ... feelin's. *(A beat. Marty rises, moves to coatrack, touches clothes, takes Cantor Levinson's robe from rack, holds it out to Joseph. Without a word, resigned, already walking with Cantor Levinson's gait, Joseph takes the robe from Marty and puts it on; he also puts on prayer shawl, a tall, white cantorial yarmulke, and a pair of rimless eyeglasses, all done with great fastidiousness.)*

MARTY. *(Seated; watching him.)* Cantor Levinson was one of the few men in the synagogue that I liked. He never raised his voice and his skin was so soft, so ... *("White" would have followed, but Marty interrupts himself.)* He'd blush at the slightest thing and his cheeks would turn into bright red apples. He probably didn't even know I was alive. It's strange. But when I was a kid I couldn't make a good impression on anyone. Not in the synagogue; not in school; not in the neighborhood. I was like the village idiot. I was always getting into trouble or it was as if I wasn't there. I didn't matter to anyone. At school I did terribly. I mean, really terribly. I couldn't pass the easiest subject. I don't know where my head was. But the minute I took off on my own, as soon as I left this house, it was an entirely different story. I did fantastically in advertising. I'm not exaggerating. Man, I was a hotshot copywriter, art director, marketing executive, right from the beginning. No one could keep up with me. No one ... *(Marty turns to Joseph. He is too dumbfounded by Joseph's appearance to continue. Joseph kisses the fringes of the prayer shawl and puts it on. In his cantorial outfit, he looks regal, absolutely splendid. He checks himself out in the mirror. Then he takes a prayer book from the box on shelf of rack. He opens it, in imitation of Cantor Levinson, solemnly, respectfully. Somehow he knows the words of a liturgical prayer, perhaps Kol Nidre, which he sings in a voice that is the best it can possibly be. It should be quite beautiful. All his gestures and movements are specifically not his own. It should be clear to us that he is not reading the prayer from the book he holds in his hands.)*

Marty listens in awe. The prayer should go on until we are truly moved by it. [There are recordings of Cantors singing liturgical prayers and the actor should listen to them to prepare for his performance.] When Joseph is done, he kisses both pages of the open prayer book before closing it. He puts back everything of Levison's where he found them. He is emotionally drained. Marty is almost without breath.) It ... It was ... beautiful. *(No response from Joseph.)* Are you all right?

JOSEPH. *(Grimly.)* You better go. I'm tired.

MARTY. Why are you sending me away? I can help you. I can ... Joe, listen to me. Please. You're being foolish. Use your head for a minute. Does your wife have everything she needs? Should she be in a hospital? I have the best internist in the country. Let me call him. Let me...

JOSEPH. There's nothing — I repeat for your benefit — there is nothing you can do except leave us alone.

MARTY. I will. Yes. I ... respect your wishes. What's so amazing to me is that I want to stay, very much, and it's not for the reasons I came here for. *(Pours cognac.)* One more drink and I promise I'm off. I'll spend the night at the Sherry-Netherlands. It'll cost me three hundred for the night. What the hell. You only pass this way once. *(A short beat.)* Joe, you sang that ... It was great. Great. I drink to your health and, despite your pessimism, to your wife's recovery.

JOSEPH. You getting a divorce?

MARTY. I haven't thought about it. Not seriously. I wouldn't want to lose my son. He's the only one in the whole Goddamn world who means anything to me.

JOSEPH. I suppose kids are easier to love than grown-ups.

MARTY. Your wife younger than you?

JOSEPH. About a year. We met in a roller-skating rink in Jamaica. My friend knew her friend and we ... we jus' took to one another. We were married a few weeks after we met. It'll be fourteen years in April. *(Shouts.)* Can you hear us, sweetheart? I'm talking to my friend, Martin Robbins, alias Rabinowitz. About our respective families. Where are your parents, Martin?

MARTY. My mother...

52

JOSEPH. *(Shouts.)* Talk louder, Martin. Elizabeth's getting a little hard of hearing!

MARTY. *(Loudly.)* My mother lives with my sister in Queens.
My father ... My father is dead.

JOSEPH. Did you hear that, sweetheart? His father is deceased!
(To Marty.) And what about the rest of your family, Martin? How
are they doing?

MARTY. I don't know...

JOSEPH. You don't know? How could you not know how your
family is doing! You used to be so close, you told me. You used to
live together, share things. *(Loudly, anguished.)* Didn't he tell me
that, sweetheart? Didn't he?

MARTY. Joe, don't...

JOSEPH. I'm jus' asking you about your relatives, Martin.

MARTY. They ... moved away. Florida, Arizona, California ... I
don't see any of them ... anymore.

JOSEPH. *(Rises; moves to coatrack where he frantically examines
clothes, looking for a particular jacket; shouts.)* He lost his family, hon-
ey! He married a young woman and he's suspicious of her feelings
for him. She says she loves him but he doesn't believe her. Can you
imagine that, sweetheart? Can you imagine two married people
worrying about something like that? *(Finally finds Marty's
grandfather's large, double-breasted jacket. He puts it on; also a 30's tie,
and old brown hat; speaks softly now.)* I'm going to take you into my
confidence, my friend Marty Rabinowitz. I am in deep, serious
trouble. Emotionally speaking I am up the creek, down the river
and 'round the bend. I have discovered, over these past couple a
months, that I cannot live in the same house with death. I have discovered that we are in-com-pat-ible and that unless I occupy my
mind elsewhere I am in an unbearable situation. *That's* what I have
discovered. *(He grabs a birchwood cane from top shelf.)* Consequent-
ly, my friend Marty Rabinowitz, I have the need, the in-dis-pen-
sable need, to lose myself in these old clothes of the old Jews. With
these clothes on me I can play hide-and-seek with my enemy. I can
fool him. I can occupy my mind. I can be ... some-body ... else.
(He hunches himself into a resemblance of Marty's grandfather. He

53

moves D., mumbling under his breath, as if praying. Shortly he turns and glares at Marty, his eyes burning vehemently, still mumbling under his breath. Marty is forced to speak.)

MARTY. *(With effort; apprehensively.)* Would you ... like to sit down ... Zada? *(A short beat before he moves to carry a chair D. for Joseph. Joseph doesn't budge.)* Can I get you anything? Is there ... anything I can do for you?

JOSEPH/ZADA. *(Glaring at Marty; in a barely hoarse voice.)* Zol ze nor kerhokit vehren!

MARTY. Who, Zada? Who are you mad at?

JOSEPH/ZADA. *In dred zol zey zein!*

MARTY. Sit down. Sit down, Zada. Please. Don't be mad. *(Leads Joseph to chair.)* You know, of everyone in my life, you're the one I wanted to talk to the most. That's the truth. That's the honest truth.

JOSEPH/ZADA. *(Seated; cane upright between thighs; still glares at Marty.)* Gay cockin off de yam!

MARTY. *(He carries another chair from table D.)* Did I ... Did I tell you I named my son after Davey, Zada? Did I ... Did I tell you I send ten thousand dollars a year to Mount Sinai Hospital in his name? You know, when he was killed in the army I was totally destroyed. He was my best, my very best friend. I loved him. And I don't ... I never blamed you for making him your favorite grandchild. I mean, I wasn't jealous, I swear. He was ... something ... special, wasn't he Zada?

JOSEPH/ZADA. *A goishea kop. Er hust a goishea kop. (Marty sits down. Joseph clasps his hands on the handle of the cane and leans his chin on his hands, staring forward.)*

MARTY. Now I'm gonna surprise you. Now I'm really gonna surprise you. Last August I sold my advertising agency. My partner and I got six-point-five for it. That means I earned, after taxes, approximately two-point-three. That's two million, three hundred thousand, clear. Plus ... Plus two-hundred-and-fifty thousand a year for five years for not working, for doing nothing!

JOSEPH/ZADA. *(Exasperatedly.)* Vos vilt er frum mer? Er macht mer meshugga!

MARTY. Are you surprised, Zada? Did you expect this of me? The truth now. Didn't you have me pegged for a loser? Didn't you think I was gonna end up like my father, a loser? a clown? someone who never amounted to anything? Didn't you think that, Zada?

JOSEPH/ZADA. *(Softly; barely hoarse voice; no inflection; improvising, not remembering.)* What do you want from me, Moishe? Why are you acting like this? I'm going. I'm going down to my own house. *(He rises and, using cane lightly, moves to door. Marty runs after him, leads him to table, bringing up chair from D.)*

MARTY. No, don't! Don't go! I'm sorry. I apologize. I won't do it again, I promise. Let's have a drink, okay? I have some terrific schnapps here. It cost me forty bucks for the bottle, no kidding. *(They sit. Marty pours cognac into two glasses.)* You know what I always remember, Zada? I remember the Sunday when the whole family was in the backyard and we were all going to the park for a picnic. I don't know how it got started but my mother said something and you said, "I'm not going! Go without me! Go! Go!" Do you remember that Sunday, Zada? *(No response from Joseph.)* That was something. Wow. Suddenly everyone was quiet. It was as if they had all turned to stone. My mother begged you to go to the park with the rest of the family. She said she was sorry. She apologized. She cried and cried, buckets of tears, buckets and buckets of tears. It seemed like hours, years before you said, "Shhh. Shhh. I'll go. We will all go." Wow, what a scene that was! The sun came out from behind the clouds. Like it was a miracle. And everyone started laughing, talking, touching one another, all at once, and my mother covered you with kisses and hugged you tightly, so tightly, the tears still pouring out of her eyes, and, and...

JOSEPH/ZADA. *(Raises his glass; chants in a strong voice.)* Boruch atoh adonoi, eleohenu melech hoolm, borah barehn agophin. *(He empties the glass in a swallow.)*

MARTY. Amen. Amen. *(He refills Joseph's glass without touching his own. Joseph leans his chin on his hands clasped on cane.)* I don't know how you did it, Zada, but your children loved you. Really, really loved you. Every single one of them. You could have asked them to run into a burning building or jump off the roof and they would have done it. And what's so amazing is that they loved you more than they loved their own families! Now I don't care what you say, Zada, that has to be a little sick. I mean, my mother married my father because you told her to, and you know that's the truth. And I have no doubt, Zada, that she would have left him on the spot if you had said the word. But what I don't understand is why you wanted her to marry him in the first place. You didn't think much of him. You didn't respect him. He was a joke to you, a *schlemiel,* an easy setup for a cheap laugh. Do you know who I was saying Kaddish for when I was a kid, Zada? It was for him. It was for my father. Because to me he was non-existent; to me he was the way you treated him, a nobody, a nothing, a dead person. And I'll tell you something else, Zada: I don't think I meant a shit to you either! I never, in all the years I lived in this house, I never recall you ever giving me an iota of affection or attention or anything. Oh, you tried to make a clown of me, like my father. You put me up on the table to sing or to imitate people or to make a jackass of myself, but nothing for me to hold onto, nothing *for me.* And you know what's so ironic? Somehow lately I've been thinking about this and I came to the bizarre conclusion that you were my real father! It figures, doesn't it? You were the man my mother went to for love and advice and everything else. Subconsciously I must have known this all along because *my* father never got what he was entitled to: my respect, my devotion, my...

JOSEPH/ZADA. *(Suddenly flares.)* Enough! Enough already! Enough questions! Enough cross-examinations! What are you carrying on about? Did I kill anybody? Did I murder anybody? You invited me to your home! Act like a man! Bring out something for the table!

MARTY. I will, Zada. I'll get...

JOSEPH/ZADA. *Oii iz dos a putz! Oii vey is meir is dos a putz!*

MARTY. What would you like? I'll get you anything...

JOSEPH/ZADA. You wouldn't have a piece of schmaltz herring in the house, would you, Moishe?

MARTY. I'm sorry. There's nothing here you'd eat. They're not kosher. I'll run down if you ... *(There is the sound of Joseph's wife ring-*

ing the tiny bell in her offstage bedroom. At once Joseph becomes grim. He removes his hat and puts it on the floor; also the cane. He rises and slowly exits to bedroom, assuming his own posture and gait. Marty watches him intently. He picks up his drink and swallows it. Joseph returns. He picks up hat and cane, sits in chair, D., stares forward, expressionlessly.) Is she ... all right? *(No answer from Joseph.)* Can I call anybody? *(A long, silent beat. Joseph awkwardly puts on hat.)*

JOSEPH/ZADA. Moishe. Moishe. Moishe. What am I going to do with you? What? What? How could you imagine such things? Was I a dictator? A Hitler? Why do you have such bad feelings for me?

MARTY. Zada, I don't...

JOSEPH/ZADA. I did my best to raise my family. I did the best I could.

MARTY. I know that. I'm not being critical.

JOSEPH/ZADA. There is anger in you, Moishe; such anger. I did not force your mother to marry your father. That is a lie. They were responsible for their own lives, not me.

MARTY. I know. I'm not taking the responsibility away from them. But you...

JOSEPH/ZADA. You talk as if there was no happiness in this house. You forget the parties, the laughter...

MARTY. That's not true. That was the first thing I said when I walked in here tonight. We did have good times, Zada. We had the best times...

JOSEPH/ZADA. Do you remember when we would go to the shul on the holidays?

MARTY. Do I remember? You have to be kidding me. How could I forget. We used to meet downstairs, all of us...

JOSEPH/ZADA. All my daughters, all my sons...

MARTY. And their daughters and their sons ... Oh, man, that was something to see. We'd walk the five blocks to the Talmus Torah, twenty, twenty-five, thirty of us, like an army we were, all dressed up in our best clothes, proud and hardly talking and holding onto each other...

JOSEPH/ZADA. All my daughters, all my sons...

MARTY. We were a good-looking family, Zada. I mean, everybody in the neighborhood used to stare at us and you could see how jealous they were, how they envied us for what we had.

JOSEPH/ZADA. We were a family, Moishe.

MARTY. We were. And it was special, and it was rare and ... *(A short beat.)* How did you get everybody in the family to love you so much, Zada? What was your secret? What was the trick? You never seemed to go out of your way or do anything for it. They just gave it to you.

JOSEPH. *(Takes off hat; in his own voice; perplexed.)* Did you hear my wife, Martin?

MARTY. *(A puzzled look.)* Who? Your wife?

JOSEPH. Did you hear her ring the bell for me? *(Marty shakes his head.)* She didn't ... ring the bell? *(Marty shakes his head. Resignedly Joseph puts the hat back on. He now speaks in the voice of Marty's grandfather. Sighs.)* You imagine too much, Moishe. I had respect for your father, may-he-rest-in-peace. To say differently is not the truth.

MARTY. I don't know how I can believe that, Zada.

JOSEPH/ZADA. You forget, I gave him my daughter. A beauty, she was. A beauty. Would I give him my daughter if I had no respect for him?

MARTY. But I can give you examples when you humiliated him in front of everybody, when...!

JOSEPH/ZADA. *(Rises; moves to coatrack for prayer book.)* Shhh. Shhh. You imagine too much. My children I loved. Each child I loved. And each grandchild I loved, without favorites.

MARTY. Without favorites? You have to be kidding me. I remember the time when...

JOSEPH/ZADA. Shhh. Shhh. We will talk. Later. Later. Tonight. Tomorrow. All week. All month. We will stay here and we will talk. About the shul. About the holidays and the parties and the laughter and the dancing ... *(He opens prayer book.)* Have you said Kaddish for your father, Moishe? *(Marty shakes his head.)* Come, we will say Kaddish. You, for your father, and I will say it for

58

... *(His eyes fill with tears; somehow he manages to hold on.)* ... for ... my wife. *(A long beat.)* And after we say Kaddish, we will talk. All week. All month. All year. As long as you wish. *(He hands Marty a yarmulke. They stand side by side, D., facing front. Joseph holds the open prayer book in front of them. He looks to the offstage bedroom before they recite the Kaddish, he from memory, Marty from the book.)*

TOGETHER. Yisgadal v'yeskadash sh'me rabbo, b'olmo deevro chiruseh v'yamlish malchuseh, b'chayochom uvyomechon, uv'chayey d'chold beys yisroel baagolo uvizman koreev, v'imrus omen. Yisborach v'yestabach v'yesp-ar v'yesroman v'yishasen v'yes-hador ... *(The light fades during the above. Blackout.)*

****

PROPERTY LIST

ONSTAGE
Enamel-topped table
3 wooden chairs
Old refrigerator
Gas range
New York Post
Pitcher of iced water (in refrigerator)
Glasses
Telephone
Medicine

OFFSTAGE
Very expensive suitcase (Marty)
Cognac (in suitcase) (Marty)
Portable coatrack (on which a line of jackets, some with prayer
        shawls on them, are hanging in a row; on the bottom shelf
        there are several pairs of shoes, some with spats, galoshes
        and rubbers; on the top shelf are a number of hats and
        skullcaps of different sizes and shapes; also 2 cardboard
        boxes, one with prayer shawls, the other with prayer
        books; a two-foot mirror hangs from top of rack, at the
        side) (Joseph)
Rimless eyeglasses (Joseph)
Birchwood cane (Joseph)

PLAYWRIGHT'S NOTE

If the producer wishes to have an evening with only two actors, then I suggest *74 GEORGIA AVENUE* be replaced by one of the following plays:

> *THE TYPISTS*
> *THE TIGER*
> (published by Dramatists Play Service:
> *THE TYPISTS and THE TIGER)*

> *A NEED FOR BRUSSELS SPROUTS*
> *A NEED FOR LESS EXPERTISE*
> (published by Samuel French, Inc:
> *TWICE AROUND THE PARK)*

> *MEMORIAL DAY*
> (published by Dramatists Play Service:
> *FIVE ONE ACT PLAYS)*

> *WALTER*
> (published by Dramatists Play Service:
> *THE PUSHCART PEDDLERS, THE FLATULIST &*
> *OTHER PLAYS)*

New

⬇⬇⬇ PLAYS

THE PERFECT PARTY

SAVAGE IN LIMBO

WRESTLERS

THE MAJESTIC KID

QUIET IN THE LAND

LILLIAN

GOODLY CREATURES

CHOPIN IN SPACE

THE COUCH

ON THE EDGE

A ROSEN BY ANY OTHER NAME

A LOVESONG FOR MISS LYDIA

DESPERADOES; THROWING SMOKE;
   KEYHOLE LOVER

INQUIRIES INVITED

DRAMATISTS PLAY SERVICE, INC.
440 Park Avenue South   New York, N.Y. 10016

New PLAYS

TENT MEETING

GOODBYE FREDDY

ANTEROOM

WAR OF THE ROSES

THE HITCH-HIKERS

THE LISBON TRAVIATA

FRESH HORSES

FULL HOOKUP

COYOTE UGLY

THE TOMORROW BOX

RAW YOUTH

MEN'S SINGLES

A BETROTHAL

DRAMATISTS PLAY SERVICE, INC.
440 Park Avenue South   New York, N.Y. 10016

RECENT

DRIVING MISS DAISY

**THE MUSICAL COMEDY MURDERS
OF 1940**

OLD WINE IN A NEW BOTTLE

THE HANDS OF ITS ENEMY

A SHAYNA MAIDEL

STRAY DOGS

THE DELUSION OF ANGELS

MARRIAGE

THE AUTHOR'S VOICE

POPS

DISCIPLES

ROAD SHOW

THE NICE AND THE NASTY

REMEDIAL ENGLISH

*Write for information as to
availability*

DRAMATISTS PLAY SERVICE, Inc.
440 Park Avenue South   New York, N.Y. 10016

0928   1990